MERCY OTIS
WARREN

AUTHOR AND HISTORIAN

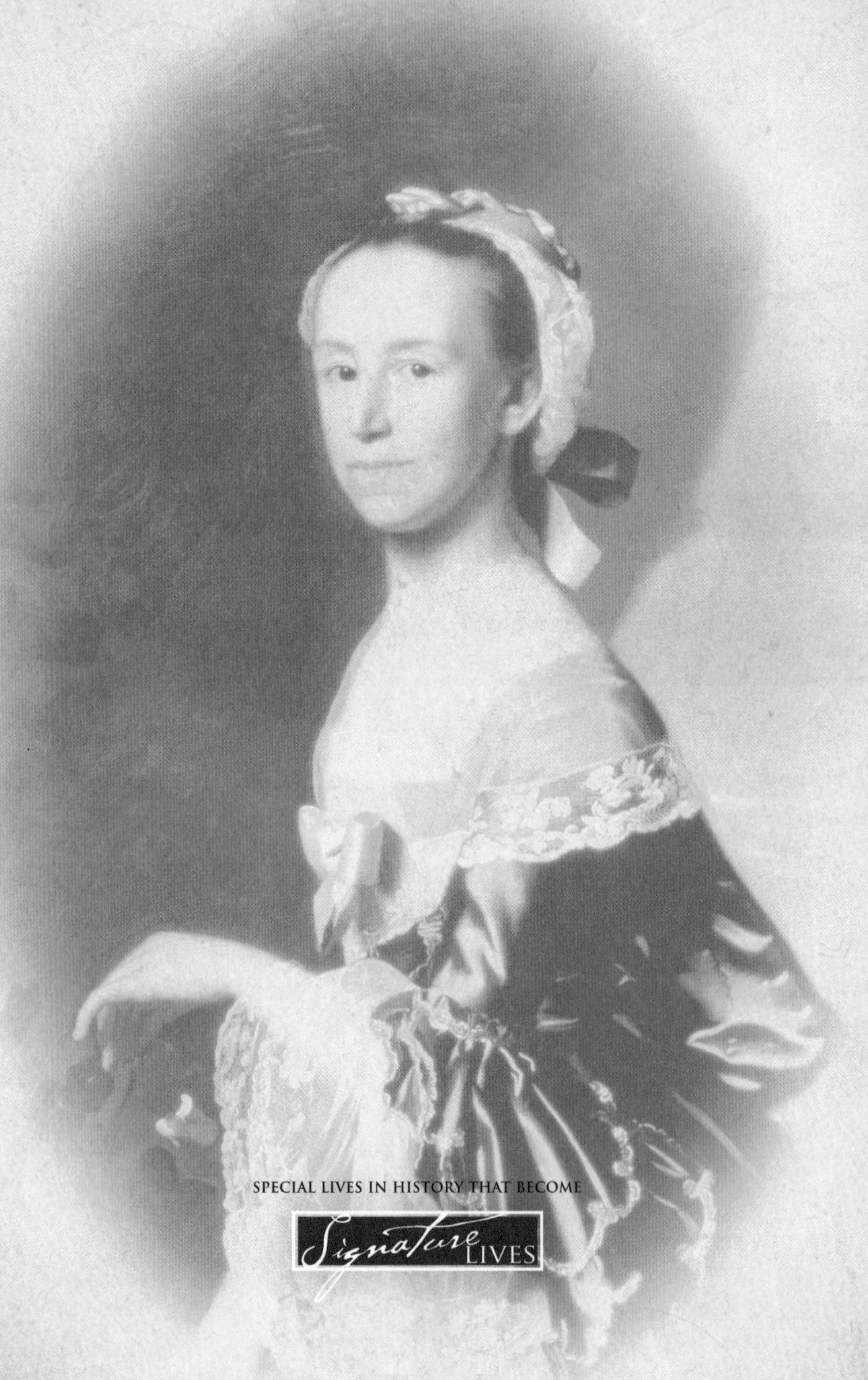

SPECIAL LIVES IN HISTORY THAT BECOME

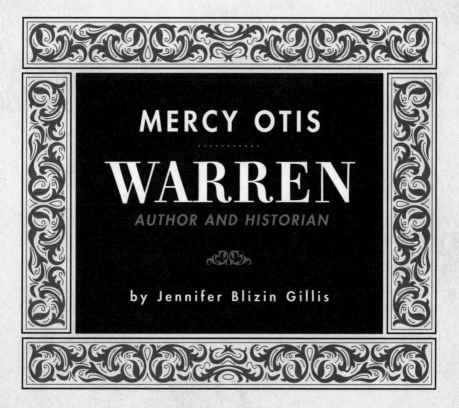

MERCY OTIS
WARREN
AUTHOR AND HISTORIAN

by Jennifer Blizin Gillis

Content Adviser: Caroline Keinath,
Superintendent, Adams National Historical Park,
Quincy, Massachusetts

Reading Adviser: Rosemary G. Palmer, Ph.D.,
Department of Literacy, College of Education,
Boise State University

COMPASS POINT BOOKS ✶ MINNEAPOLIS, MINNESOTA

Compass Point Books
3109 West 50th Street, #115
Minneapolis, MN 55410

Visit Compass Point Books on the Internet at *www.compasspointbooks.com*
or e-mail your request to *custserv@compasspointbooks.com*

Editor: Sue Vander Hook
Lead Designer: Jaime Martens
Page Production: Noumenon Creative
Photo Researcher: Svetlana Zhurkin
Cartographer: XNR Productions, Inc.
Educational Consultant: Diane Smolinski

Managing Editor: Catherine Neitge
Creative Director: Keith Griffin
Editorial Director: Carol Jones

Library of Congress Cataloging-in-Publication Data
Gillis, Jennifer Blizin.
   Mercy Otis Warren / by Jennifer Gillis
      p. cm. — (Signature Lives)
   Includes bibliographical references and index.
   ISBN-13: 978-0-7565-0982-8 (hardcover)
   ISBN-10: 0-7565-0982-3 (hardcover)
   ISBN-13: 978-0-7565-1865-3 (paperback)
   ISBN-10: 0-7565-1865-2 (paperback)
   1. Warren, Mercy Otis, 1728-1814—Juvenile literature. 2. United
States—History—Revolution, 1775-1783—Biography—Juvenile literature.
3. Authors, American—18th century—Biography—Juvenile literature. 4.
Historians—United States—Biography—Juvenile literature. I. Title. II.
Series
PS858, W8G55 2006
973.3'092—dc22   2005002706

REVOLUTIONARY WAR ERA

The American Revolution created heroes—and traitors—
who shaped the birth of a new nation: the United States of
America. "Taxation without representation" was a serious
problem for the American colonies during the mid-1700s.
Great Britain imposed harsh taxes and refused to give the
colonists a voice in their own government. The colonists
rebelled and declared their independence from Britain—
the war was on.

Table of Contents

Chapter 1
AN END AND A BEGINNING

❧❧❧

Mercy Otis Warren was stunned when the messenger told her the awful news. The night before, her 44-year-old brother, James Otis, was beaten in a Boston coffeehouse. The fight started with an argument between Otis and John Robinson, a customs official in charge of inspecting goods going in and out of Boston Harbor in Massachusetts. The quarrel turned violent, and somehow, the candles and lamps went out. In the darkness, Robinson and his friends pounded Otis with their canes, causing extremely serious injuries to his head.

Mercy was in Plymouth, Massachusetts, about 40 miles (64 kilometers) south of Boston, when she received the news on that September day in 1769. It was too far to rush to her brother's side, and the trip

James Otis (1725-1783) was a lawyer and one of the main political leaders in Massachusetts in the mid-1700s.

would have been difficult with her five young sons. Instead, Mercy dashed to her writing desk and did what she had done many times before. She wrote a letter to her beloved brother, pouring out her feelings on paper. As her pen flew across the page, she didn't take time to date it. She wrote, "My dear Brother: You know not what I have suffered for you." In her poetic style, she made the letter sound like she had witnessed the beating. She imagined that her brother had died.

I saw you fallen—slain by the hands of merciless men—I saw your wife a widow, your children orphans.

Otis did not die from the beating, but he was never the same. This brilliant speaker and lawyer would never think very clearly again. He would still be a patriot who spoke out against the way England was ruling the American colonies, but his words would not have the same effect. He had often encouraged Mercy to think about political issues. Their letters to each other were full of opinions and new ideas. In 1766, three years before the beating, Otis was bold enough to write that without liberty, he didn't want to live in the colonies.

Otis had a gift for words and was able to convince people that British laws were unfair. He made many colonists realize they were paying too many taxes and that they should at least have a vote in the British Parliament. They had to obey whatever decisions the king of England and Parliament made. In newspaper articles, pamphlets, and speeches, Otis spoke out against unfair taxes and the limited rights of the colonists. He planted the seeds that grew into

British soldiers arrest an American colonist shortly before the Revolutionary War.

a war for independence—the Revolutionary War.

Unfair British laws were on the minds of many colonists at that time. In 1765, Britain had passed the Stamp Act, forcing colonists to pay for a stamp on every piece of paper that was circulated. Newspapers, wills, deeds, and more had to bear a stamp. Otis and others spoke out against this act, and many colonists agreed. Britain repealed the Stamp Act in December of the same year, but soon other taxes and laws were passed.

Mercy agreed with her brother's stand on British rule. But she didn't give speeches and attend meetings to discuss her complaints. In the mid-1700s, women were expected to tend to home and children, not get involved in politics. Mercy was an intelligent woman, though, and her brother respected her for that. Together, they discussed the issues and corresponded about solutions to the grievances the colonists had against Britain.

Now that James Otis had lost much of his mental ability to fight for the cause of colonial freedom, Mercy became stronger in her fight. Her brother's political career was ending, but hers was just beginning. She would not speak in court or become a government official, but she would influence people with her ideas and writings.

Using pen and paper, she would affect people with powerful letters, plays, poetry, and pamphlets.

She didn't write for entertainment; she wrote to persuade people to challenge the British government. She influenced colonial leaders and advised them how to take action. Her ideas and suggestions shaped the country and gave her a place as one of the founding mothers of the nation.

Mercy Otis Warren finished her emotional letter to her injured brother, whom she fondly called Jemmy. "Thousands are thanking you and ... praying for your recovery," she wrote. On that September evening, Mercy picked up where her brother left off. One patriot's work was done; another's was just beginning. 🕮

James Otis was declared legally incompetent in 1771.

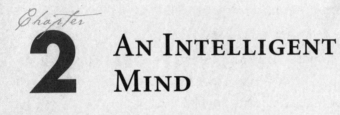

2 AN INTELLIGENT MIND

Chapter

❦

Mercy Otis Warren was 41 years old when her brother Jemmy was beaten. Although they both had their own families, they had remained close friends throughout the years. Jemmy once wrote to Mercy, "No man ever loved a sister better."

Jemmy was the oldest of seven Otis children. When Mercy was born on September 25, 1728, Jemmy was 3 years old, and her other brother, Joseph, was 2. Their father, Colonel James Otis, was a busy man, who worked as a farmer, lawyer, judge, politician, military officer, and merchant in the city of Barnstable, Massachusetts. Their mother, Mary Alleyne Otis, came from a respected and wealthy Massachusetts family.

The Otises' large, comfortable house overlooked

Portrait of Mercy Otis Warren by John Singleton Copley, famous American artist of the colonial period the low-lying salty waters of Cape Cod on the Atlantic Coast, where small fishing villages and farms dotted the land. Many people were farmers, whalers, fishers, and shipbuilders. It was a special place for these Massachusetts colonists, whose grandfathers and grandmothers had stepped off the *Mayflower* on that shore in 1620. Those pilgrims started the second English settlement in America— Plymouth Colony, which later came to be known as the Massachusetts Bay Colony.

The pilgrims lived a simple life based on their strong religious beliefs that were based on the standards of the Bible. Prayer, preaching, and Bible reading were important to them. Working hard was essential, and duty came before having fun. They started their own church, the Congregational Church, where the Otises attended every Sunday. The Otis family had strong religious beliefs and lived the simple life of their ancestors.

Although they lived quite modestly, the Otises were

The Puritans, or Pilgrims, were the original settlers of Massachusetts. Their society was based on contracts called covenants. Puritan covenants stressed a personal responsibility to the rest of the group and had strict rules for dress and behavior. Ministers were powerful rulers who could force people to leave the colony if they broke the covenant. The Congregational Church grew out of the Puritan religion. Although it became a little less strict, plain living and good behavior were still important.

Pilgrims at church in Plymouth, Massachusetts

wealthy. Inside their house was furniture imported from Europe. Most colonists sat on rough hand-made chairs and slept on mattresses stuffed with straw, but Mercy's family had expensive chairs, soft feather beds, and silver dishes. They even had mirrors and a clock, things only wealthy people could afford at that time. But the Otises didn't show off their riches by wearing fancy clothes or having big parties. Every member of the family was expected to work and keep the farm and household running smoothly, even though they had several servants and a slave.

Mercy learned to do the things that girls were supposed to do in colonial America. She cooked, sewed, and learned how to run a household, but she preferred spending time with her brother Jemmy and her father. Colonel Otis wanted the best for his children. He provided a good education for his sons by hiring a tutor to teach them. The Reverend Jonathan Russell, a local minister and graduate of Harvard College, was given the job.

Girls did not receive a formal education at that time, but Colonel Otis didn't mind when 9-year-old Mercy started going along with her brothers to their lessons. As Russell taught, Mercy listened attentively, taking special interest in lessons about the history of the world. Poems and plays also interested her, especially those by famous English writers. She had a smart mind, and her father encouraged her to learn.

When Mercy and Jemmy weren't studying, they spent a lot of time together. They talked about what they were learning, what was happening in their colony, and politics. Most likely, they knew about politics from their father, who was very involved in Barnstable's government. Mercy often listened to her father and his friends talk about how

A colonial schoolmaster and his pupils

Massachusetts was being ruled by the British. She heard how the colony had to do whatever the king of England decided.

Mercy's lively conversations with her brother were interrupted in 1740, however, when he went to Harvard College in Cambridge, Massachusetts. But

Mercy and Jemmy didn't stop communicating. Now they wrote letters, often about the books they were reading. Her favorite was *A History of the World* by Sir Walter Raleigh.

Three years later, Jemmy graduated from Harvard. Fifteen-year-old Mercy was invited to go to the graduation ceremonies with her parents. It was her first trip away from home. The Otises probably went by boat to Boston, the biggest city in the American colonies at that time. Then they went on to Cambridge by carriage, where Mercy got her first glimpse of Harvard, the first college established in the colonies. It was already more than 100 years old, founded in 1636 by the Pilgrims just 16 years after they arrived at Plymouth. Most Harvard graduates at that time became ministers in the Puritan churches throughout the colonies.

After graduating, Jemmy returned to Barnstable with his family, where he studied for his master's degree. He also taught Mercy many things he had learned at school.

But in two years, he left again. This time, he went to Boston to become a lawyer. Since there were no law schools, he had to learn the law by working and studying with an experienced lawyer. Jemmy worked with Jeremiah Gridley, one of the best lawyers in Massachusetts. Gridley belonged to a political party called the Whigs, which took sides

18th-century engraving of Harvard College as it looked in 1767

with the colonists when they complained about how the British were governing the colonies.

About that time, Mercy's father was elected to

Colonel James Otis had seven children; three of them rose to prominence during the Revolutionary war—James, Mercy, and Samuel.

the Massachusetts House of Representatives, a group of men who helped make laws for the colony. His position often required him to be away from home at meetings.

With Jemmy gone and her father away so often, Mercy had no one to talk to about books or politics. She was not close with her sisters or her mother, so she kept in touch with Jemmy and her father through letters. After spending two years in Boston,

Jemmy moved closer to home in nearby Plymouth, where he opened a law office.

James Warren, one of Jemmy's Harvard classmates, also lived in Plymouth. From time to time, James and Jemmy visited the Otises in Barnstable. Mercy may have already known James from her visit to Harvard. But she wouldn't have known then how their relationship would grow and what an important part he would play in her life. ✍

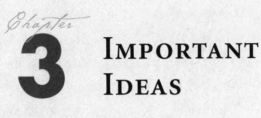

3 IMPORTANT IDEAS

ᕫᕫᕫ⟡ᕫᕫᕫ

Mercy Otis thought James Warren was a smart man with a lot of promise. He had been a good student at Harvard, and he had strong feelings about how the colonies should be governed.

Warren lived with his family on their large farm in Plymouth, Massachusetts, along the Eel River. The Warrens were a very prominent New England family. James' grandfather came to Plymouth in 1620 onboard the *Mayflower*. His father was a very successful businessman, who traded goods with companies overseas. He was also the sheriff of Plymouth County, captain in the local military, and a government representative for Massachusetts.

James and Mercy had a lot in common, and they shared a lot of the same ideas. They both thought

A Puritan couple on their way to church

women and men were equal. In those days, nearly everyone believed that men were smarter, stronger, and better at everything. James was different. He appreciated Mercy's bright mind, and Mercy enjoyed keeping up with the men intellectually. At times, however, she seemed a bit uncomfortable with her intelligence. To her friend Abigail Adams she once wrote, "Men nor women were not made to think alike—it cannot be." Later, she wrote in another letter that it was probably better for women to let their

Some colonial children were taught in a dame school, which met in a home and was taught by a mother or grandmother.

husbands be in charge of everything in order to keep peace in the house.

At that time, most people thought too much reading was harmful to a woman's mind. Most men didn't want to marry a woman who was outspoken or acted educated. Fortunately for Mercy, the men in her life—her father, Jemmy, and now James Warren—did not think like most people. They made her feel as though her ideas were just as important as any man's.

They all agreed on political issues, as well. Jemmy and James studied government together at Harvard. They especially liked the ideas of John Locke, an English writer who had died in 1704. He wrote that the job of government is to help and protect the people. When their leaders mistreat them or do not help them, then people should have a right to choose someone else to govern them. These were new thoughts for most colonists, but the idea of a government for the benefit of the people was becoming more and more popular.

English philosopher John Locke (1632-1704)

Most girls in New England learned how to read. This was because the Puritan religion taught that everyone should be able to read the Bible. If young children went to school, they went to a dame school, where children gathered at someone's house to learn. Children who grew up on farms were often taught by their parents, since a dame school might be many miles away. It was not unusual for someone to be able to read but not write. Often, girls were taught to write only their names.

Mercy's relationship with James Warren soon grew deeper, and in 1748, they became engaged. After an unusually long engagement of six years, the couple was married in November 1754. Mercy was 26 years old, and James was 28. Since Congregationalists did not believe in church weddings, James and Mercy were married by a judge at the Otises' house.

At first, Mercy and James lived with his family on their farm along the river. But in 1755, they bought their own house in Plymouth. It faced the town square, not far from the spot where the Pilgrims landed. However, they didn't live there very long. In 1757, James' father died and left him the farm and his position as sheriff.

The couple moved back to the Warren family home. That same year, Mercy gave birth to their first child, named James after his father. Over the next nine years, she and her husband had four more sons—Winslow, Charles, Henry, and George.

Mercy raised their five sons and ran their

The Atlantic shore at Plymouth, Massachusetts

household well. Her views on discipline were somewhat different than what her church taught. Congregationalists believed that children should work hard and be quiet. Any other behavior was punished, usually with a spanking, to prevent children from becoming spoiled or selfish. Mercy had other ideas about children. She called them tender plants and thought parents should pay attention to the good things they did. She believed parents were examples and should behave the way they wanted their children to act.

Although Mercy gave a lot of her time to her children, she also took time to read, study, and write. Often, she wrote letters to her friends, sometimes giving advice on raising children. She also wrote poetry. In 1759, the year Winslow was born, Mercy wrote and published her first poem titled, "On Winter."

In the midst of raising a family, Mercy didn't forget about sharing her political ideas. She had the unusual ability to keep up with her duties as a wife and mother and also take part in the political world of the men. She still corresponded often with her brother Jemmy, who was back in Boston now and married to Ruth Cunningham.

John Adams
(1735-1826)

Mercy's and Jemmy's letters were often about the changes taking place in the colonies. People were beginning to think more about breaking away from British rule. Jemmy's young friend, 20-year-old John Adams, wrote in 1755 that all of Europe would not be able to hold back the colonies.

But the British Parliament was not letting colonists break away. In fact, Parliament was giving more government positions to British rulers. Massachusetts colonists weren't happy when Thomas Hutchinson was appointed in 1757 to the

Governor's Council, a group of lawmakers hand-picked by the British governor of Massachusetts to rule the colony. Most people thought Colonel Otis would be chosen for the council position. Otis even gave up his position in the Massachusetts House of Representatives because he thought he would be moving up to the more powerful council position. But the governor appointed Hutchinson instead.

The British Parliament made laws for England and the American colonies.

The Otis family grew to detest Hutchinson. Mercy wrote:

> *He was dark, intriguing, insinuating*
> *[sneaky], haughty, and ambitious, while*
> *the extreme of avarice [greed] marked*
> *each feature of his character.*

The Otises didn't like the way he rose to power so quickly and took away Colonel Otis' chance to serve on the council. Otis and Hutchinson didn't agree on politics, either. Hutchinson believed in strong British rule, while Otis thought the colonists should have a say in what laws were passed.

Parliament was not happy to hear that the colonists wanted more say in government. In fact, the British sensed a rebellion and started enforcing old laws and making stricter ones. The old Navigation Act of 1651 was one that Parliament decided to start enforcing. It required colonists to ship all goods through England before they could ship merchandise to another colony. The law also required all goods coming into America to pass through England first.

The colonists were strongly against the way Britain was restricting their businesses. For years, colonists just ignored the Navigation Act and smuggled foreign goods into the country. Sugar, molasses, rum, and other supplies often were unloaded from ships at night to avoid British officials.

All colonial cargo had to go through British customs agents at the London Customs House on the River Thames.

The colonists became more outspoken, and Great Britain became more difficult. Americans questioned the rights of the British government, and the British Parliament passed more laws for the colonies. James and Mercy Warren's home became a meeting place for American patriots who believed the colonies should be able to rule themselves.

Leading patriots met in Mercy's living room to discuss their complaints against Britain, and they talked about possible solutions. Mercy shared her ideas with the men who attended. She often used her knowledge and intelligence to influence these people who soon would become the leaders of a revolution. 🔊

4 TROUBLE BREWS

Chapter

❧❧❧❧

The British were determined to control the rebellious colonists. First, they had to find out who was hiding smuggled goods. The Writs of Assistance allowed the British to enter colonists' homes and businesses without warning. If anything appeared to be smuggled merchandise, the British took it. They not only seized goods, but they damaged American ships. One ship that belonged to the wealthy John Hancock family was destroyed. The colonists were outraged.

That same year, in 1760, Thomas Hutchinson again used his power to take another position away from Mercy's father. Massachusetts needed a new chief justice, the highest judge in the colony. As an experienced, well-known lawyer,

Thomas Hutchinson (1711-1780), a loyalist, was hated by the patriots who supported independence from Britain.

Colonel Otis was a strong candidate, but Hutchinson was given the position. The Otises were furious. Hutchinson already was a member of the Governor's Council, a county judge, and lieutenant governor of the colony. Now he was chief justice, too.

In February 1761, the colonists brought their complaints against the British before five judges in a Boston court. The judge in charge was Thomas Hutchinson. The lawyer for the colonists was Mercy's brother, Jemmy. The lawyer for England was Jeremiah Gridley, who had trained Jemmy to be an attorney.

The courtroom was packed with patriots and loyalists, who were still loyal to England. Jemmy's friend, John Adams, was there, writing down notes about what was going on. Gridley spoke out in support of Britain's right to search for smuggled goods. Jemmy spoke out for the rights of the Boston merchants in a fiery speech that lasted five hours.

That day, Mercy's 35-year-old brother planted the seed of patriotism in America and openly opposed British rule for the first time. The fight for freedom had begun, and Mercy's brother was one of the ones responsible. He was the first voice of independence and was soon nicknamed "the patriot." Mercy was proud of Jemmy's passionate, fiery courtroom speech.

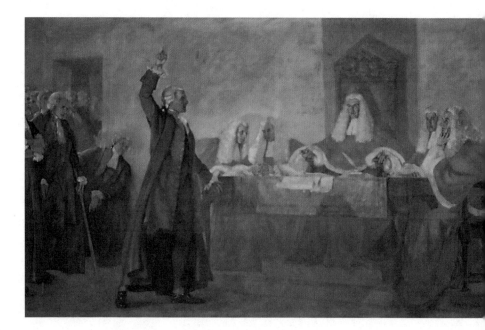

She later wrote:

> *He was the first champion of American freedom. ... He had in a clear, concise, and daring manner stated ... the rights of the American Colonies.*

James Otis protests the British Writs of Assistance, which empowered customs officials to search anywhere, even in houses, for smuggled goods.

Any decision Hutchinson made in court that day would put him in a difficult position. If he agreed with American merchants, he might lose favor with the king. If he decided in favor of British laws, he would become unpopular with the rich merchants of Massachusetts. So he delayed his decision, and the case was never settled.

But the case turned many Boston merchants

against Hutchinson, and they questioned Britain's rights even more. Jemmy continued to work hard for freedom. He and his father began writing letters and articles against Hutchinson and publishing them in Boston newspapers. Jemmy criticized Hutchinson and Britain harshly in 1764 in a pamphlet, a powerful booklet that encouraged the patriot cause. Hutchinson grew to hate Jemmy.

Customs officials who checked for smugglers also hated Jemmy, because now they had a hard time enforcing the Navigation Act. Colonists kept on doing business like they always had, ignoring the unpopular British laws.

Mercy joined the fight for freedom, too, although in a much quieter way than her forceful brother. Between 1757 and 1764, meetings in the Warren home happened more and more frequently. Leaders of the patriot cause came there to talk about the growing problems with the British. Mercy didn't hesitate to make her home available or to share her political opinions with the men at these meetings.

Among the patriot leaders who came to Mercy's home were friends like John Adams and his cousin Samuel Adams. John Adams was not surprised that Mercy participated in their political discussions. Adams' wife, Abigail, was also interested in politics and often wrote letters to people about the situation in the colonies. Abigail and

Mercy often corresponded about everything from politics to French plays and the price of soap.

The Warren household was often abuzz with talk about new laws, such as the Sugar Act of 1764. This law put a new tax on sugar, coffee, and certain wines and cloth. In 1765, many colonists were talking about the Stamp Act that had just passed. Under this law, colonists had to pay a tax on every piece of paper they used, from newspapers to legal documents and playing cards. Each paper had to be stamped to show that the tax had been paid.

British soldiers patrolled Boston Harbor, Massachusetts, to make sure the colonists were not smuggling goods.

The colonists were furious and angrily protested in the streets. Mercy wrote, "The lower classes broke out into ... riot and tumult." In some cities, people handed out printed flyers and rang bells to protest the new tax.

Once again, Jemmy stirred up the people of Boston. He wrote newspaper articles accusing Hutchinson of supporting the Stamp Act. An angry mob formed, encouraged by a group of radical patriots called the Sons of Liberty. The group turned violent and destroyed Hutchinson's house and all his belongings. Hutchinson barely escaped with his life.

Although Thomas Hutchinson was born in Boston, he preferred the British way of life. He dressed like a British dandy, a man concerned with an elegant appearance. People said he was very proud and arrogant. When government jobs opened up, Hutchinson made sure that his friends or family members got them.

At a gathering at Mercy's home, a small group of patriots decided there should be a meeting of representatives from all the colonies to discuss the new taxes. The meeting was organized, and people from each colony met in New York City, where they wrote a formal request to England's King George III, asking him to repeal the Stamp Act.

While the representatives were waiting for the king's reply, James Warren was elected to the Massachusetts House of

Representatives and began spending more time away from home. Although Mercy sometimes traveled to Boston to visit her husband, she usually stayed at home in Plymouth with the children.

Mercy missed James and was upset that he was

The Sons of Liberty attacked Thomas Hutchinson's house on August 26, 1765.

away from home so much. In her loneliness, she wrote a poem to him, titled "To J. Warren, Esq.: An Invitation to Retirement." In her poetic style, she asked James to give up politics and come back to their quiet life on Cape Cod. Mercy was dedicated to the patriot cause, but she wasn't sure she was willing to give up that much time with her husband.

The British repealed the Stamp Act on March 18, 1766, just one year after it had gone into effect. There were celebrations throughout the colonies. People thought their troubles with Great Britain might be over. But a few like John Adams, Samuel Adams, and James Otis still didn't trust the British. They didn't trust England and knew the British would not back down quite that easily.

As suspected, the British soon found another way to tax the American colonies. They passed the Townshend Acts in 1767, forcing colonists to pay taxes on things like glass, lead, paint, paper, and tea. They also taxed silk, lace, and

The colonists' outrage over the Stamp Act sparked the beginning of an organization called the Sons of Liberty. Samuel Adams was most likely the organizer of this group, although he was careful not to take part in their activities. The Sons of Liberty often tried to scare British officials so they would be afraid to do their jobs. One way they frightened British leaders was by hanging stuffed dummies that looked like them from an old oak tree in Boston. The tree came to be known as the Liberty Tree.

British stamps were sold for a variety of prices according to the value of the printed document.

other fancy materials used to make clothes for the wealthy.

Once again, Mercy's home in Plymouth became a

meeting place for angry patriots. Mercy took part in one meeting, recommending a solution to the Townshend Acts. She suggested that they write letters and send them throughout all the colonies. The letters would urge colonists to boycott British goods, refusing to buy anything made in England. Colonists would make their own cloth and find a substitute for English tea. If they couldn't make something themselves, they would just get along without it.

The idea was called the Committees of Correspondence, and soon many letters started circulating from colony to colony. Mercy wrote that the letters "expressed the boldest determination to continue a free but loyal people." By boycotting British-made merchandise, the colonists would not be paying any taxes to England, and they also would not be breaking any laws.

The boycott was a huge success, especially with women. They stopped buying things made in England and organized spinning bees, where women got together to spin yarn and thread to make home-made cloth. They exchanged recipes for "Liberty Tea," a drink made with the leaves of colonial-grown herbs. In some cities, patriots embarrassed people who continued to buy British goods by publishing their names in the newspaper.

Britain was very unhappy that the colonists

Colonists used spinning wheels to turn fibers into thread or yarn, which they wove into cloth to make clothes.

found a way to avoid paying taxes. The king was furious, and he would not allow the Massachusetts House of Representatives to meet any longer. He sent warships full of soldiers to Boston. Many people blamed Jemmy Otis for Great Britain's warlike actions. Otis had worked very hard to stir up the people against the British government and his enemy, Thomas Hutchinson.

Loyalists, also called Tories, sometimes insulted Otis openly on the streets of Boston. They published articles in the newspaper that made fun of him and even wrote a nasty song about him called

"Jemmibullero." Although his friends advised him not to pay attention to the insults, Jemmy found himself thinking about his enemies night and day. He wrote and published an advertisement in a newspaper naming his enemies and demanding that they stop insulting him.

No one knows why Otis went to a coffeehouse alone one September night in 1769. He knew his enemies were there. It was no surprise to anyone when an argument broke out between Otis and several British customs officials. The hatred between these officials and Jemmy was no secret. The men became angry and beat Otis violently in the head with their canes.

Jemmy's brain was severely damaged from the blows to his head that night, and he was never the same brilliant speaker or patriot for independence again. After the attack, he began wandering the streets of Boston. Two years later, he was declared legally incompetent. Mercy wrote to a friend:

> *It is indeed hard ... to see those abilities ...*
> *clouded, shattered, and broken: to see the*
> *mind of a man so superior thus darkened,*
> *and that man a most affectionate brother,*
> *is grief beyond expression.*

Perhaps Jemmy's ability to fiercely fight the patriot cause was over, but Mercy would take over where her brother left off. ☙

GOVERNMENT
A
POWER DELEGATED
FOR THE
HAPPINESS
OF
MANKIND
CONDUCTED
BY
WISDOM
JUSTICE
AND
MERCY

5   A MIGHTY PEN

Chapter

❧❧❧

As Jemmy Otis got worse, his family tried to help him. He went to live with his father in Barnstable, but Colonel Otis was getting too old and too ill to handle Jemmy's sudden outbursts. At times, Jemmy became so violent that his brother Joseph had to hold him down. The only person who could calm him was Mercy, so Jemmy moved into her house.

Mercy helped Jemmy as best she could. He had written many letters to people over the years, and people continued to write to him, but now he was unable to answer them. So Mercy began answering his mail for him. One letter she answered was from Catharine Macaulay, a writer who lived in England and supported the colonists in their struggles with Britain.

Catharine S. Macaulay (1731-1791), English writer and historian

After Mercy told Macaulay about the attack on Jemmy, the two women began to correspond regularly. Little did the women know that they would write to each other for the next 18 years. "Dear Madam," their letters always began. Mercy and Catharine shared a common interest in history and politics. Catharine often encouraged Mercy to publish her poems and writings. They usually corresponded about the colonies and what was happening in America.

Things were not calm in the colonies, especially in Boston. People were angry that increasing numbers of British soldiers were constantly patrolling their streets. Colonists made fun of these soldiers in red uniforms, calling them redcoats, lobsterbacks, and other insulting names. In March 1770, violence broke out in the city, and five colonists were killed in what came to be called the Boston Massacre.

In 1771, the British government became disgusted with the governor of Massachusetts and blamed him for allowing the colonists to riot and protest in the streets. The governor was ordered to return to England. Thomas Hutchinson, the Otis family's greatest enemy, became governor of Massachusetts. If Jemmy had been well, he probably would have churned out an angry pamphlet in protest. But "the patriot" was no longer able to bother Hutchinson. With the encouragement of Catharine Macaulay,

Mercy decided to do what Jemmy would have done if he had been able.

Mercy was angry that Hutchinson now was governor of Massachusetts, and she fought with her pen and paper. In 1772, she wrote a play about a cruel government led by a British-appointed Massachusetts governor named Rapatio. Of course, the governor was Hutchinson, but Mercy attacked him in her own secret way. Her brother was one of the heroes. His name in the play was Brutus, the name of an honest, patriotic senator of

Angry colonists and British soldiers opened fire in front of the State House in Boston, Massachusetts, on March 5, 1770, in what came to called the Boston Massacre.

ancient Rome. The play took place in Upper Servia, the name she used for Boston.

The play was not meant to be acted out on a stage. In Puritan society, theater productions were not allowed. Mercy's play was written so people would read it, enjoy the story, and receive a strong political message at the same time. Parts of Mercy's play were published in a Boston newspaper, the *Massachusetts Spy*, on March 26, 1772. In April, more of the play was printed. In 1773, the entire play, called *The Adulateur*, was published in a pamphlet.

The play was anonymous, with no author's name. Mercy had to be careful. After all, it was against the law to write or speak against the British government. She didn't use her own name, and she didn't use people's real names in the play. Instead, she gave her British foes the names of ancient Greek and Roman gods. People could read between the lines to figure out that Rapatio was really Hutchinson. *The Adulateur* was very popular. John Adams was its biggest supporter and was probably responsible for getting it published. He was one of the few people who knew that Mercy Otis Warren was the author.

On May 24 and July 19, 1773, parts of Warren's second play, *The Defeat*, appeared in the *Boston Gazette*. Evil Rapatio and honest Brutus were back,

Popular hatred for Thomas Hutchinson, governor of Massachusetts Colony, was expressed in a 1774 cartoon.

along with a long list of other characters. In the end, Rapatio and his followers were conquered. What Mercy was really saying was that the patriots would defeat the loyalists. But they would not reach their final goal—independence for America.

This time, more people knew that Mercy was the writer of the play. *The Defeat* became so popular that it was reprinted in newspapers in New York and Philadelphia. *The Adulateur* and *The Defeat* both helped many colonists change their minds about

In a pamphlet called "The Rights of the British Colonists Asserted and Proved," Jemmy Otis wrote, "Taxation without representation is tyranny." Many people read this pamphlet and were influenced by it. "No taxation without representation!" became a popular expression before the Revolutionary War.

staying loyal to Great Britain. Mercy's brother Jemmy had used anger and fiery language in his pamphlets, but Mercy got her point across with humor and fictional characters to encourage people to change their points of view.

Colonists were becoming more and more bold. The first test of their courage came in 1773, when the British passed the Tea Act, a law that tried to force colonists to buy British tea. Several colonies held so-called "tea parties" and destroyed chests of British tea. In December, a group of Massachusetts patriots dressed up like Mohawk Indians and boarded a British ship in Boston Harbor for the largest tea party yet. More than 90,000 pounds of tea were thrown into the harbor that day in what came to be called the Boston Tea Party. This was their way of protesting the tea tax. Boston's patriots were thrilled with the success of their huge tea party. The British government was outraged.

John Adams called the Boston Tea Party "a bold and daring act." In a letter to James Warren, Adams said he wished someone would write a poem about

The Boston Tea Party, December 16, 1773

it. A month later, a humorous poem called "The Squabble of the Sea Nymphs" appeared in the *Boston Gazette*. It told the story of a fight between two wives of the sea god Neptune. One wife who stood for British loyalists wanted to keep tea on land. The other wife represented the colonists, and she wanted the tea for the "gods of the waters." In the end, Indians threw the tea into the water. Mercy's name wasn't on the poem, but many people knew she was the writer.

Mercy Warren's plays and poetry were powerful tools that influenced the colonists. But equally powerful were her letters to leading patriots of the day. She and John Adams corresponded often. They both were very outspoken and did not try to hide their opinions. They sometimes carried on disagreements in their letters. But even when they did not agree, they remained friends.

Mercy's friendship with his wife, Abigail, continued to grow stronger, too. Abigail was 13 years younger than Mercy, but they shared the same viewpoints on many issues. They both wanted America to be independent, and they both wanted women to have more rights. Both of their husbands were often away at meetings, so they frequently shared their feelings about managing a household, raising children alone, and solving political issues.

In 1774, Britain passed the Coercive Acts, which the colonists called the Intolerable Acts, in an attempt to stop the

Abigail Adams and Mercy Warren wrote letters to each other for several years before they finally met in 1773. An early believer in women's rights, Abigail wrote to her husband, John, while he was making plans for the new nation. She asked him to "remember the ladies."

Abigail Adams (1744-1818), wife of John Adams and mother of John Quincy Adams

colonists from rebelling. The British Parliament thought these new strict laws would frighten people and make them more obedient. Instead, colonists were troubled and angry. Now, they had to feed British soldiers and let them live in their homes. British ships patrolled Boston Harbor so no

A VIEW OF THE TOWN OF BOSTON WITH SEVERAL SHIPS OF WAR IN THE HARBOUR.

British warships in Boston Harbor in 1774 attempt to control the angry colonists.

American ships could go in or out. Only British ships were allowed passage. Goods sold in stores had to be made in England. In addition, British colonial officials accused of wrongdoing could be sent to England for trial, so they could do whatever they wished in the colonies without fear of reprisal.

Word soon spread that a representative from each colony should go to Philadelphia, Pennsylvania, for a meeting. Fifty-six representatives from 12 of the 13 colonies met in Philadelphia for the First Continental Congress in September 1774. Most of them were also members of the Committees of Correspondence. Members of the Continental Congress wrote a statement that the colonies were not going to obey the Intolerable

Acts. They also said they would no longer buy or sell British goods. Each colony would also train soldiers and have their own militia.

At the suggestion of a friend, Mercy again picked up a pen and wrote a humorous but very meaningful poem called "To the Hon. J. Winthrop, Esq." In the poem, two selfish women named Clarissa and Prudentia are busy buying imported feathers, furs, satin, silver, and porcelain. Their patriotic friends, on the other hand, are doing without. Of course, the heroes of Mercy's poem are the patriotic friends.

As lighthearted as Mercy's writings seemed, the deeper meanings were heavy on her heart. She and most other colonists knew that independence for the colonies would not come easily. Conflicts between the colonists and the British were growing, and many people knew that war most likely was unavoidable. As 1775 drew near, Mercy continued to write about the events taking place. She started writing a new play about the colonists' pursuit of freedom. Her play would affect the patriots who wanted freedom so much. It might even spark the beginnings of a war. ஒ

Chapter

6 WAR!

❧✦❧

The *Boston Gazette* published parts of Mercy Warren's new political play, *The Group*, on January 23, 1775. Three days later, the *Massachusetts Spy* printed parts of it. Many of the characters were outspoken women, who represented the patriots and Tories. The play made fun of British officials governing Massachusetts. It hinted that anyone who supported Britain was corrupt and cared only about money.

The names of some of the Tory characters—Simple Sapling and Crusty Crowbar—showed just how weak they were. The play ends with a Tory woman making a final speech that leaves a character named Freedom weeping onstage.

The play was a huge success. That year, it was

printed as a political pamphlet and distributed throughout Boston, Philadelphia, and New York City. Angry patriots were encouraged by the play to keep working for freedom. Freedom would not be left crying on their "stage." They were ready to fight for independence.

In April 1775, the British government declared that Massachusetts was in a state of rebellion. Thomas Gage, who recently had taken Thomas Hutchinson's place as governor of the colony, was also the general in charge of the British army. He ordered his soldiers to go to Concord, Massachusetts, to visit Colonel James Barrett's farm. He heard that colonists were storing cannons, muskets, powder, and other weapons there. Gage's orders were to destroy the weapons and capture rebel leaders Samuel Adams and John Hancock in nearby Lexington.

Thomas Gage (1721-1787), British general and colonial governor

Word spread that the British were coming. One patriot, Paul Revere, arranged for signals to be sent by lantern from the steeple of Christ Church, now called Old North Church, in Boston. One lit lantern meant the British were coming by land; two meant they were coming by sea. On the night of April 18, 1775, two lanterns were lit. Patriots rode through towns on horseback to warn citizens. Revere took the north route, and William Dawes took the south.

Early on April 19, about 700 British soldiers got off their boats in knee-deep water in Boston Harbor and began their march. When they entered Lexington, 77 colonial soldiers were waiting for them. Shots were fired. Eight Americans died and 10 were wounded. Only one British soldier was hurt. The Revolutionary War had begun.

British troops continued to Concord, where more than 300 colonial minutemen had gathered. The colonists watched silently as British soldiers

The British retreat from Concord under fire from colonial minutemen.

marched into town on their way to search the Barrett farm. Most of the weapons had been removed by the time the British arrived. On their return march, the British were attacked by rebel troops. Soldiers on both sides were killed, and the battle spread out over two miles (3.2 km). Finally, the exhausted British reached their warships in Boston.

On June 16, 1775, the redcoats marched up Breed's Hill in nearby Charlestown in one long, powerful row. The rebels had planned to fight the British on Bunker Hill but changed their minds at the last minute and moved to nearby Breed's Hill.

Jemmy Otis was there with them, hunkered down behind a makeshift stone wall. Somehow, he had found a gun and made his way to the battlefield. The injuries to his brain six years before left him unable to think clearly, but he managed to stay alive through the fierce fighting. He survived what came to be called the Battle of Bunker Hill.

James Warren was nearby that day, too, serving as a general in the Massachusetts militia. On June 18, he wrote from Watertown to his wife, Mercy:

> *With a Savage Barbarity never practised among Civilized Nations they fired & have Utterly destroyed the Town of Charlestown. ... it is Impossible to describe the Confusion in this place, Women & Children flying into the Country, armed Men Going to the field, and wounded Men returning from there fill the Streets.*

He also told her about Jemmy, who "borrowed a gun and went among the flying bullets." He told her how Jemmy later sat down for dinner with him, but then got up and wandered off before the meal was over.

Mercy worried about her family's safety. Jemmy was not well, and James was near the fiercest battles. She wondered how safe her son James was at Harvard College. Mercy also worried about her four sons who were still at home. They were just 9, 11, 13, and 16 years old, and Plymouth was not the safest place to be in Massachusetts. Many people were loyalists and did not get along with the patriots. Mercy was afraid her strong patriot family might be attacked. She and the boys left Plymouth for a while, but returned when she realized how dangerous it was throughout the entire colony.

James Warren was torn. The country needed his help, but he loved his family deeply and was worried about Mercy. When the British finally pulled out of Boston and headed to New York City, James left the army and went home. He was offered a position on the Massachusetts Supreme Court but turned it down, because he would have to be away from home too much. Some patriot leaders began to think of James Warren as a quitter. Many people were making huge personal sacrifices for the cause of freedom.

It was not uncommon for wives to be separated from their husbands for long periods of time. Abigail Adams managed their farm and household alone for years while John Adams worked for independence for the colonies. Abigail wrote to Mercy in 1775:

> *I find I am obliged to summon all of my patriotism to feel willing to part with him again. You will readily believe me when I say I make no small sacrifice to the publick.*

Mercy was not so willing to be apart from James. She wrote to Abigail that she was not willing to give up her husband to the state for long periods of time. Mercy didn't demand that James stay home, but she quietly expected him to be there most of the time.

On July 4, 1776, the colonists officially declared their independence with the Declaration of Independence. The document was written by Thomas Jefferson and signed by 56 representatives from all 13 colonies. That same month, a huge British force arrived in New York, determined to crush the rebellion. But General George Washington, the new leader of the colonial Continental Army, fought back fiercely, unwilling to give up despite the difficulties of the battle.

George Washington taking command of the Continental Army

Map Legend:
- 🟆 American victory
- 🟆 British victory

CANADA

Quebec, 1775

Lake Superior

Montreal

St. Lawrence River

Mass.

Fort Ticonderoga, 1777

Fort Ticonderoga, 1775

N.H.

Lake Ontario

Concord, 1775

Saratoga, 1777

Albany • Lexington, 1775

Bunker Hill, 1775

Boston

Lake Huron

Lake Michigan

Lake Erie

N.Y. Conn.

Mass.

Newport, 1778

R.I.

Pa.

Trenton, 1776

Battle of Long Island, 1776

Germantown, 1777

Princeton, 1777

Valley Forge •

N.J.

Brandywine Creek, 1777

Md. Del.

Ohio River

Appalachian Mountains

Virginia

Richmond •

Yorktown, 1781

Atlantic Ocean

BRITISH NORTH AMERICA

Guilford Courthouse, 1781

N.C.

Mississippi River

Kings Mountain, 1780

Cowpens, 1781

Camden, 1780

Wilmington

S.C.

Charleston, 1780

Georgia

Proclamation Line of 1763

Savannah, 1778

N
W — E
S

| 0 | 200 miles |
| 0 | 200 kilometers |

West Florida

East Florida

Several battles of the Revolutionary War took place in Massachusetts.

A few weeks before, Mercy visited with the general's wife, Martha Washington. In a letter to Abigail Adams, Mercy wrote all the details of their meeting, including the exact time of the visit. Mercy was also busy writing another play. *The Blockheads* was published in Boston in 1776. In this humorous story with a serious meaning, she boldly portrayed the British as fools.

As the war raged on over the next four years, Mercy wrote more and more. The power of her pen made her a strong influence in the war. She wrote forceful letters and published more political plays and pamphlets. She also started writing down details of what was happening in the war. She continued to correspond with patriot leaders, discussing the war and the beginnings of a new independent nation. She encouraged John Adams to tell people not be frightened and to keep on fighting.

Mercy was very respected for her political views, but she was always careful not to go too far. She knew there was a certain line that women did not cross in those days. In one letter to Adams, she asked his forgiveness for "touching on war, politicks, or any thing relative thereto … so far beyond the line of my sex."

The remaining years of the war would bring many changes for the Warren family. As the country changed, so would their friendships with many of the leaders. ✒

Chapter

7 YEARS OF GRIEF

❧❀❧

As the war dragged on over the next four years, James and Mercy Warren started disagreeing with many of their friends. They felt leaders of the new nation were grabbing for power.

Younger friends like John Hancock and John Adams were given high positions in the new government, but James Warren was left out. In 1778, he lost the election for the Massachusetts House of Representatives. Mercy began to have bitter feelings toward old friends who were now enjoying great success.

Some people who had been farmers or merchants before the war made fortunes selling food and supplies to the Army. Mercy and James were shocked to see them put on airs and imitate the manners and dress of British nobles. Mercy published two poems in the *Boston Gazette* newspaper that accused Americans of worshiping gold and going against the very principles for which they were fighting. She also wrote two plays, *The Sack of Rome* and *The Ladies of Castile*, which humorously criticized the newly formed United States. The plays suggested that a love of luxury would destroy the young country.

Many people didn't agree with Mercy and James. Even their second son, Winslow, rebelled against his parents' principles. He refused to go to Harvard, as his older brother James had done. Instead, he moved to Boston and lived a wild life, drinking too much, wasting money on stylish clothes, and running up big gambling debts.

Winslow wrote his mother a letter, telling her how much he liked a book he had read about a father who advised his son to think only of himself. If that meant cheating friends, he wrote, so be it, as long as he was true to himself.

Mercy was horrified. She felt that Winslow was betraying everything she had taught him. She wrote him a strong reply, warning him that this book "honeyed poison," meaning it made evil seem good. She sent a copy of her letter to Abigail Adams, who thought it was so good that she had it published in the newspaper.

*Winslow
Warren, second
son of James
and Mercy
Warren*

After his wild stay in Boston, Winslow planned a
move to Europe. On the way, the British captured his
ship and took him prisoner. When he was set free, he

The Seine River in Paris, France

went to France, a country Mercy thought of as an evil, sinful place. She wrote him a poem, "To a Young Gentleman, Residing in France," warning him about trying to live a life of luxury. She asked him to come home and closed the poem with the line:

Return, my son, for nothing else we need,
To see thee happy, would be bliss indeed.

The life Winslow chose troubled Mercy and James. They had also been deeply saddened when their oldest son James was wounded in the Revolutionary War. He had joined the navy after finishing at Harvard. In a battle with a British warship, his leg was severely wounded and had to be amputated. He returned home as an invalid and spent the rest of his life helping his mother at home.

There was also bad news about Mercy's third son Charles. He had tuberculosis, a disease of the lungs that usually killed people. Mercy and James sent him to Spain, where the warm weather might help his condition. They wanted him to live with Winslow, who was there looking for a job. But soon, after Charles' ship set sail for Spain, Winslow showed up at home. He had left Europe without telling his parents. Who would Charles live with in Spain? As it turned out, Charles was so sick that he died on the ship before it ever landed in Europe.

Winslow went back to Boston. He continued living a wild life and soon owed people large sums of money for gambling debts. He borrowed money to pay them off and then beat up the man who loaned him the money. He wound up in a special debtor's prison for people who could not pay back the money they owed.

Meanwhile, George, the youngest of the family, moved to

Henry Warren was the only son of James and Mercy Warren to have a family of his own. He married Polly Winslow in 1791, and they had eight children. In 1800, when Thomas Jefferson was elected president of the United States, Henry Warren was appointed customs collector for the port at Plymouth, Massachusetts.

Maine to start a farm, and Mercy missed him very much. Then in 1783, Mercy received bad news about her brother Jemmy. This great speaker and patriot had died. The unfortunate beating he had received at the hands of customs officials earlier in his life had caused him to experience many years of aimlessness and insanity. After living for a while with Mercy, he had moved in with a friend and finally with his younger brother Samuel in Andover, not far from Boston.

The end of his life came in a bizarre way. He once said to Mercy that he hoped he would be taken into eternity by a flash of lightning. On May 23, 1783, Jemmy was leaning against the door of his brother's home as he watched a storm. A bolt of lightning darted from the sky and passed through his body.

John Adams wrote in his diary about James Otis:

> *I have been young and am now old, and I solemnly say I have never known a man whose love of his country was more ardent and sincere, never one who suffered so much.*

As she had always done, Mercy expressed her feelings and sadness through her writings. She wrote poems celebrating the lives of her son Charles and her dear brother Jemmy. In letters to family members and friends, she poured out her deepest sorrows.

The Boston Almanack *featured James Otis on the cover.*

This period of sorrow was mixed with conflicts the Warrens were having with friends. Thoughts of an old enemy, Thomas Hutchinson, came back in 1783. The Warrens heard that Hutchinson's large, expensive home near Boston was for sale. Mercy and James could not pass up the chance to buy their rival's house.

That same year, in September, the United States signed a peace treaty with Britain, officially ending the Revolutionary War. This should have been a time of celebration for 55-year-old Mercy and her husband. They had spent years working for the patriot cause, and now it was finally over. But her heart was heavy with all the sorrows she had endured.

The signing of the Treaty of Paris in 1783 marked the official end of the Revolutionary War.

She gathered together everything she had written over the years. She collected the letters she had received from leaders of the new nation like John

Adams, Thomas Jefferson, and George Washington. She read over letters from Abigail Adams, Catharine Macaulay, Martha Washington, and her friend Hannah Winthrop, who had witnessed the brutal battle at Lexington. She organized her own notes on the war and recalled the conversations of patriot leaders that had taken place in her living room.

Her collection was a vivid history of the nation's long struggle for independence. Then, she started putting all the information into a book. For the next 25 years, she worked on a project that would become the first history book written by an American woman. ℘

Chapter

8 A NEW NATION

∼⟨⟩∼

While the Warrens were struggling with personal problems, the United States was struggling with a new government. The 13 colonies suddenly had to work together as a nation. Mercy Warren compared the country to a child who was not mature enough to handle too much freedom. The Articles of Confederation, approved in 1781, explained how the government was supposed to work, but the laws were weak. Government did not have the power to tax the people. Each state had to tax its citizens and share the money with the government. Some states refused to do this.

Some people didn't want to pay taxes at all. In 1786, Massachusetts farmers rose up and fought rather than pay taxes. There was no national army,

A mob of discontents seize the Massachusetts courthouse during what came to be called Shays' Rebellion.

so Massachusetts had to ask other states to send soldiers to help stop the fighting. What came to be known as Shays' Rebellion spread to other states and lasted until 1787.

Mercy and James Warren felt sorry for the farmers and understood their reasons for not wanting to pay taxes. Rumors began to spread that the Warrens supported Shays' Rebellion. This made the Warrens even more unpopular.

In 1787, representatives from each state met at the State House in Philadelphia to write a constitution for the United States. Laws and standards for the entire nation might prevent disagreements between the states. Representatives at the Constitutional Convention got off on the wrong foot by not allowing citizens to attend the meeting or hear what they were doing. Many people thought the new government had something to hide.

The new Constitution of the United States was finally finished, but some people weren't happy with

> *The farmers of western Massachusetts felt they were being asked to pay more than their fair share of taxes. They also felt they were not fairly represented in state government and claimed that the tax was taxation without representation. A farmer named Daniel Shays organized many of them into a military group. The struggle became known as Shays' Rebellion. James and Mercy Warren's son Henry served with the Massachusetts militia when it was sent to help put down the rebellion.*

George Washington presides at the Constitutional Convention at Philadelphia in 1787.

it. All the states had to approve it, and the country was divided. The Federalists supported the Constitution, and the anti-Federalists were against it. This was the beginning of political parties in the United States.

Patriots like James and Mercy Warren, Samuel Adams, Patrick Henry, and Thomas Jefferson were against the new Constitution. They thought it gave too much power to just a few people. What if the government became unreasonable? They felt there was nothing in the Constitution that guaranteed people's rights.

Now, James Warren turned to writing to try to influence people. His essays criticized the Constitution, but few people saw things the way he did. Leaders of the country considered the opinions of the Warrens and Samuel Adams to be old-fashioned. They wrote against James Warren in the newspapers, and Samuel Adams received death threats. It nearly ended the Warrens' friendship with John and Abigail Adams, who didn't agree with James and Mercy. They rarely corresponded or talked for nearly 20 years.

In 1788, a pamphlet called *Observations on the New Constitution* was published. It stated reasons why the states should not ratify the new Constitution. People wondered who wrote it. The author was just "A Columbian Patriot." The ideas were so well developed that few suspected a woman had written it. But the author was a woman—the very intelligent, 60-year-old Mercy Otis Warren. John Adams knew she was the author. In fact, when people claimed she couldn't have written it, he went to court and signed a paper swearing that she was the author.

The framers of the Constitution decided to end some of the conflict over the new document and add a Bill of Rights. These were promises that the people of the United States had certain rights that the government could never take away. On May 23, 1788, the last states ratified the Constitution, and it went into effect in 1789. Most Americans, including Mercy and James Warren, agreed to support the Constitution and the new government. But the country's leaders, especially John Adams, never forgot the Warrens' attempts to turn the states against the Constitution.

With the foundations of the new nation in place, Mercy now concentrated more on writing. In 1790, at the age of 62, she published a collection of her writings. For the first time, her name was on it as the author. *Poems, Dramatic and Miscellaneous*, by Mrs. M. Warren, contained two plays she had written during the Revolutionary War. It also contained some of her political poems. It made Mercy famous, and she got many letters of congratulations from old friends, including John Adams. But her pride and happiness were soon overshadowed by a terrible tragedy.

Mercy and James had worked hard to keep their son Winslow out of trouble. At the age of 32, he had already been in jail twice and had never had a permanent job. Mercy wrote letters to friends who held important government offices, asking them to find a job for Winslow. She wrote John Adams, who was now the first vice president of the United States. He was insulted and wrote Mercy that even if he had the power to get jobs for people, he wouldn't do it. He did not want to do a favor for the unpopular Warrens.

The following year, in 1791, Winslow joined the Army and went west to help protect the new frontier settlements in Ohio. Soon after, he was killed in a battle between the settlers and the Indians. For a while, Mercy was so saddened that she could not write.

Two of her sons were now dead. Another son had lost his leg, and her youngest son was far away in Maine. Her beloved brother was gone, and her good friend Catharine Macaulay had died. Sometimes Mercy spent all day in bed, overwhelmed with grief. She grew bitter and began speaking out against the Federalists. While most people admired and honored George Washington, Mercy blamed the nation's first president for Winslow's death. She reasoned that if Washington had not sent soldiers to the frontier, Winslow would not have been killed.

Mercy's eyesight had been getting worse for

Vermont

New Hampshire

New York

Merrimack River

Quabbin Reservoir

0   30 miles
0   30 kilometers

N
W   E
S

Connecticut River

Massachusetts

Boston

Plymouth

Connecticut

Rhode Island

Barnstable

Atlantic Ocean

some time, but now she was having trouble reading and writing. Her son James, who still lived at home, helped her get through this difficult time. When letters came from enthusiastic people who had read her works, James read them aloud to his mother. Mercy replied to the letters by telling James what to write. It was James who would help her finish her ongoing project—a three-volume history of the Revolutionary War. ✍

Mercy Otis Warren lived her entire life in Barnstable and Plymouth, Massachusetts.

MERCY
OTIS
WARREN
BORN W BARNSTABLE
1725 ——— 1814

CHAMPION OF THE BILL OF RIGHTS
PLAYWRIGHT · POET · HISTORIAN
PATRIOT

MASS DAUGHTERS OF THE AMERICAN REVOLUTION

9

Chapter

SHARING HISTORY

⤜⧽⟆⧼⤛

In 1805, Mercy Warren finished writing her American history book. The three-volume *History of the Rise, Progress, and Termination of the American Revolution* had 31 chapters and more than 1,200 pages. It told many exciting details of the Revolutionary War.

At that time, a book was not printed until enough people agreed ahead of time to buy it. It took a long time before enough people wanted to buy Mercy Warren's book. Perhaps it was because the war had been over for more than 20 years, and other history books had already been published. Also, the Warrens still weren't highly respected after their opposition to the Constitution.

Mercy's book described many of the famous

Statue of Mercy Otis Warren in front of the Barnstable County Superior Courthouse in Barnstable, Massachusetts people involved in the war. She wanted her readers to see the people who fought for freedom and who started the United States as human beings, not as heroes. She wrote about George Washington:

> *[He] was a gentleman of family and fortune, of a polite, but not a learned education; he appeared to possess a coolness of temper, and a degree of moderation and judgment, that qualified him for the elevated station in which he was now placed.*

Present at the signing of the Declaration of Independence were John Hancock, Benjamin Franklin, John Adams, and others.

She described John Hancock, one of the signers of the Declaration of Independence, as "a young gentleman of fortune, of more external accomplishments than real abilities." She portrayed Benjamin Franklin as friendly and polite. But she described General Charles Lee, third in command

under General Washington, as ugly and sloppy with bad manners.

Instead of maps and diagrams of battles, she gave vivid details that other history books didn't have. She also wrote about the women of the young nation. It was very unusual at that time for books to include information about women. She had no kind words in her book for the British and portrayed the soldiers as monsters who even attacked loyalists.

One person who bought Mercy's book was very unhappy with it. In 1807, John Adams wrote an angry letter to Mercy, complaining about the way she criticized him. His letter started a heated con-flict that lasted for seven years.

Thomas Jefferson (1743-1826)

Adams said he was embar-rassed for Mercy because her book was so full of mis-takes. She fired back, saying Adams should be embarrassed for being so self-cen-tered. He accused her of writing the book to get in the good graces of Thomas Jefferson, who was now the third president of the United States. She wrote back saying

Adams was disgusting and she felt sorry for him. He insulted her by calling her a scribbler and saying that women had no business writing history books. The insults continued, and in Mercy's sixth and final letter, she demanded that Adams apologize to her. He refused.

The following year, on November 28, 1808, James Warren died at the age of 84. Many friends wrote to Mercy to express their sorrow. John and Abigail Adams kept silent. Mercy grieved for her husband, and she honored his life in a poem published in the *Boston Gazette*. The first letter of each line combined to spell J-a-m-e-s W-a-r-r-e-n.

Elbridge Gerry (1744-1813) was one of the signers of the Declaration of Independence.

Three years passed, and in 1811, an old family friend, Elbridge Gerry, came to visit Mercy. Gerry had been at many of the patriot gatherings at the Warrens' house and had lived for a while in France to help negotiate a peace treaty with Great Britain. Now he was the governor of Massachusetts and a friend of John Adams. He begged Mercy to apologize and end her feud with John and Abigail Adams.

Although she would not apologize, Mercy told her son James what to write down in a letter to John Adams. She told Adams she wanted to forget their disagreement. The letter did not mend their differences right away, but it did heal the friendship between Mercy and Abigail.

Abigail responded to Mercy with a friendly letter, and a year later, she visited Mercy in Plymouth. The two women exchanged locks of hair, a common expression of friendship in those days. Mercy and John Adams finally began writing to each other again, exchanging once again their political views and their concerns about a new war, the War of 1812.

Abigail Adams, wife of John Adams, the second president of the United States

Although Mercy was nearly blind and very frail, she was still in good health. Her mind was very sharp, and she never stopped learning and studying. In her last years, she kept up with politics and knew how the young nation was growing and being recognized throughout the world.

She continued to have James write her letters for her. She wrote to old friends like Elbridge Gerry

The War of 1812 between the United States and Britain was fought for freedom of the seas. The United States government complained that the British were interfering with American shipping. The United States successfully stopped the British from capturing Baltimore, Maryland, and New Orleans, Louisiana. In the end, neither side won the war, but they both claimed victory.

and to new friends like young John Quincy Adams, the son of John and Abigail. One day, he would become the sixth president of the United States.

In October 1814, Mercy suddenly became ill. For four days, she was in great pain. Finally, on October 19, 1814, at her home in Plymouth, Massachusetts, Mercy Otis Warren died. She was 86.

A true patriot had passed away. In her letters, plays, and volumes of history, she left behind a fascinating glimpse of the Revolutionary War era and the beginnings of a new nation.

Although it was unusual for women at that time to be involved in politics, Mercy Otis Warren contributed to the ideas of independence and encouraged the patriot cause at meetings in her home.

Her intelligent ideas and powerful writings urged many colonists to seek independence from Britain. Once the Revolutionary War began, she supported those who fought for freedom and disgraced the British government in her writings. She fought for her newly formed country, not with weapons, but with her pen and a piece of paper.

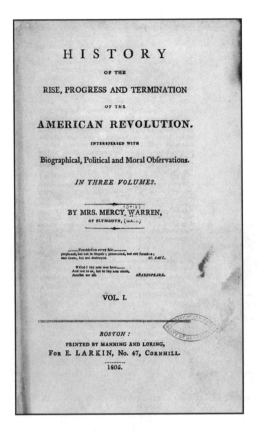

Mercy Otis Warren's history of the Revolutionary War was published in three volumes in Boston in 1805.

Mercy Otis Warren will long be remembered for what she wrote and for the account of history that she left. But she will also be remembered as one of the great women who helped lay the foundation for the United States of America.

1735

Tutored by the
Reverend
Jonathan
Russell

1728

Born in
Barnstable,
Massachusetts,
September 14

1730

1738

Englishman
John Wesley
and his brother
Charles found
the Methodist
Church

1726

Jonathan Swift
publishes
Gulliver's Travels

1754

Marries James
Warren; lives in
Warren family
house in Plymouth,
Massachusetts

1757

Son James
is born

1759

Son Winslow
is born;
writes poem,
"On Winter"

1755

1749

German writer
Johann Wolfgang
Goethe is born

1759

The British
Museum opens
in London

WARREN'S LIFE

1765
Husband James
is elected to
Massachusetts
House of
Representatives

1762
Son Charles
is born

1764
Son Henry
is born

1760

1764
James Hargreaves
creates the
spinning jenny,
a mechanical
spinning wheel

1762
Catherine the Great
becomes empress of
Russia and rules for
34 years

WORLD EVENTS

1766

Son George is born; writes poem, "To J. Warren, Esq.: An Invitation to Retirement"

1769

Brother James Otis is beaten in Boston coffeehouse

1772

Selections from first play, *The Adulateur*, appear in newspaper

1770

1768

British explorer James Cook leaves England for a three-year exploration of the Pacific Ocean

1770

Clergyman and chemist Joseph Priestly gives rubber its name when he discovers it rubs out pencil marks

WARREN'S LIFE

1773

Second play,
The Defeat,
is published
in several
newspapers

1775

The Group, a
political play, is
published in
newspapers and
as a pamphlet;
Revolutionary
War begins

1788

Writes
pamphlets
and articles
against new
Constitution

1780

1774

King Louis XV of
France dies, and his
grandson, Louis XVI
is crowned

1783

The first manned
hot air balloon
flight is made in
Paris, France, by the
Montgolfier brothers

WORLD EVENTS

1805

History of the Rise, Progress, and Termination of the American Revolution is published in Boston

HISTORY
OF THE
RISE, PROGRESS AND TERMINATION
OF THE
AMERICAN REVOLUTION.

Biographical, Political and Moral Observations.

IN THREE VOLUMES.

BY MRS. MERCY WARREN,
OF PLYMOUTH, (MASS.)

VOL. I.

BOSTON:
PRINTED BY MANNING AND LORING,
For E. LARKIN, No. 47, Cornhill.
1805.

1808

Husband James Warren dies

1814

Dies in Plymouth, Massachusetts, October 19

1810

1809

Louis Braille of France, inventor of a writing system for the blind, is born

DATE OF BIRTH: September 14, 1728

BIRTHPLACE: Barnstable, Massachusetts

FATHER: James Otis

MOTHER: Mary Alleyne Otis

EDUCATION: No formal education

SPOUSE: James Warren

DATE OF MARRIAGE: November 1754

CHILDREN: James (1757-?)
Winslow (1759-1791)
Charles (1762-?)
Henry (1764-?)
George (1766-?)

DATE OF DEATH: October 19, 1814

PLACE OF BURIAL: Plymouth, Massachusetts

IN THE LIBRARY

Burgan, Michael. *Great Women of the American Revolution*. Minneapolis: Compass Point Books, 2005.

Furbee, Mary R. *Women of the American Revolution*. San Diego, Calif.: Lucent Books, 1999.

Kallen, Stuart A. *Life During the American Revolution*. San Diego, Calif.: Lucent Books, 2002.

Silcox-Jarrett, Diane. *Heroines of the American Revolution: America's Founding Mothers*. New York: Scholastic, 2000.

LOOK FOR MORE SIGNATURE LIVES
BOOKS ABOUT THIS ERA:

Abigail Adams: *Courageous Patriot and First Lady*

Samuel Adams: *Patriot and Statesman*

Ethan Allen: *Green Mountain Rebel*

Benedict Arnold: *From Patriot to Traitor*

Benjamin Franklin: *Scientist and Statesman*

Alexander Hamilton: *Founding Father and Statesman*

John Hancock: *Signer for Independence*

John Paul Jones: *Father of the American Navy*

Thomas Paine: *Great Writer of the Revolution*

Martha Washington: *First Lady of the United States*

Phillis Wheatley: *Slave and Poet*

On the Web

For more information on *Mercy Otis Warren*, use FactHound to track down Web sites related to this book.

1. Go to *www.facthound.com*
2. Type in a search word related to this book or this book ID: 075650982-3
3. Click on the *Fetch It* button.

FactHound will find the best Web sites for you.

Historic Sites

Barnstable County Superior Courthouse
Barnstable, MA 02630
508/362-9484
To see the Mercy Otis Warren statue and the statue of her brother, James Otis

Pilgrim Hall Museum
75 Court St.
Plymouth, MA 02360
508/746-1620
To view Mercy Otis Warren's needlework and the dress she wore the day after her wedding

anti-Federalists
colonists who were against a strong central government and wanted individual rights included in the U.S. Constitution

boycott
to refuse to do business with someone as a form of protest

customs officials
people who make sure people pay taxes on imported or exported goods

elegy
a poem expressing sorrow for one who has died

Federalists
colonists who favored a strong central government and supported the U.S. Constitution

loyalists
colonists who remained loyal to the British government

militia
citizens who have been organized to fight as a group but who are not professional soldiers

minutemen
colonists who were ready to fight at a moment's notice

pamphlet
a small booklet

Parliament
the part of the British government that makes laws

patriot
American colonists who wanted their independence from Britain

Puritans
religious group that moved to New England to
protest against the Church of England

radical
having extremely different views about politics

smallpox
viral disease that causes people's skin to break
out in blisters and leaves deep scars

Tories
colonists who remained loyal to the British
government

tragedy
a play that is very sad and in which one or more
characters die

tyranny
government in which all the power is in the hands
of one ruler, who keeps people in their place by
using threats

Chapter 1

Page 10, line 11: Jeffrey Richards. *Mercy Otis Warren.* New York: Twayne Publishers, 1995, p. 116.

Page 13, line 16: Katharine Susan Anthony. *First Lady of the Revolution: The Life of Mercy Otis Warren.* Garden City, N.Y.: Doubleday, 1958, p. 71.

Chapter 2

Page 15, line 4: *Mercy Otis Warren*, p. 7.

Chapter 3

Page 26, line 8: Mercy Otis Warren. *Letter to Abigail Adams*, 1807.

Page 32, line 3: Mercy Otis Warren. *History of the Rise, Progress, and Termination of the American Revolution.* Boston: Manning and Loring, 1805. Reprint Indianapolis, Ind.: The Liberty Fund, 1994.

Chapter 4

Page 37, line 2: John Clarke Ridpath. "James Otis the Pre-Revolutionist." *Great Americans of History.* http://www.samizdat.com/warren/jamesotis.html.

Page 40, line 2: Rosemarie Zagarri. *A Woman's Dilemma: Mercy Otis Warren and the American Revolution.* Wheeling, Ill.: Harlan Davidson, 1995, p. 54.

Page 44, line 14: *History of the Rise, Progress, and Termination of the American Revolution*, p. 28.

Page 47, line 13: *A Woman's Dilemma: Mercy Otis Warren and the American Revolution*, p. 54.

Chapter 6

Page 67, line 1: "June 18, 1775 Letter From James Warren to Mercy Otis Warren." *The Massachusetts Historical Society*, www.masshist.org/bh/warrenp1text.html, p. 1.

Page 66, line 13: http://chnm.gmu.edu/courses/zagarri/hist499/students/farish.html#fn9.

Page XX, line X: Ibid.

Chapter 7

Page 74, line 6: Melissa Bohrer. *Glory, Passion, and Principle.* New York: Atria, 2003, p. 113.

Page 76, line 18: Ibid.

Chapter 9

Page 90, line 5: *History of the Rise, Progress, and Termination of the American Revolution*, p. 128.

Page 90, line 12: Ibid., p. 116.

Adams, Charles F., ed. *Correspondence Between John Adams and Mercy Warren*. New York: Arno Press, 1972.

Bohrer, Melissa. *Glory, Passion, and Principle*. New York: Atria, 2003.

Anthony, Katharine Susan. *First Lady of the Revolution: The Life of Mercy Otis Warren*. Garden City, N.Y.: Doubleday, 1958.

Bohrer, Melissa Lukeman. *Glory, Passion, and Principle: The Story of Eight Remarkable Women at the Core of the American Revolution*. New York: Atria Books, 2003.

Franklin, Benjamin, ed. *The Plays and Poems of Mercy Otis Warren*. Delmar, N.Y.: Scholars' Facsimiles and Reprints, 1980.

Richards, Jeffrey H. *Mercy Otis Warren*. New York: Twayne Publishers, 1995.

Roberts, Cokie. *Founding Mothers: The Women Who Raised Our Nation*. New York: William Morrow, 2004.

Warren, Mercy Otis. *History of the Rise, Progress, and Termination of the American Revolution*. Boston: Manning and Loring, 1805 Reprint. Indianapolis, Ind.: The Liberty Fund, 1994.

Zagarri, Rosemarie. *A Woman's Dilemma: Mercy Otis Warren and the American Revolution*. Wheeling, Ill.: Harlan Davidson, 1995.

Jennifer Blizin Gillis writes poetry and nonfiction books for children. She first became interested in history while living near Fredericksburg, Virginia, close to many battlefields. She lives on a former dairy farm in Pittsboro, North Carolina, with her husband, a dog, and a cat.

Image Credits